Contents

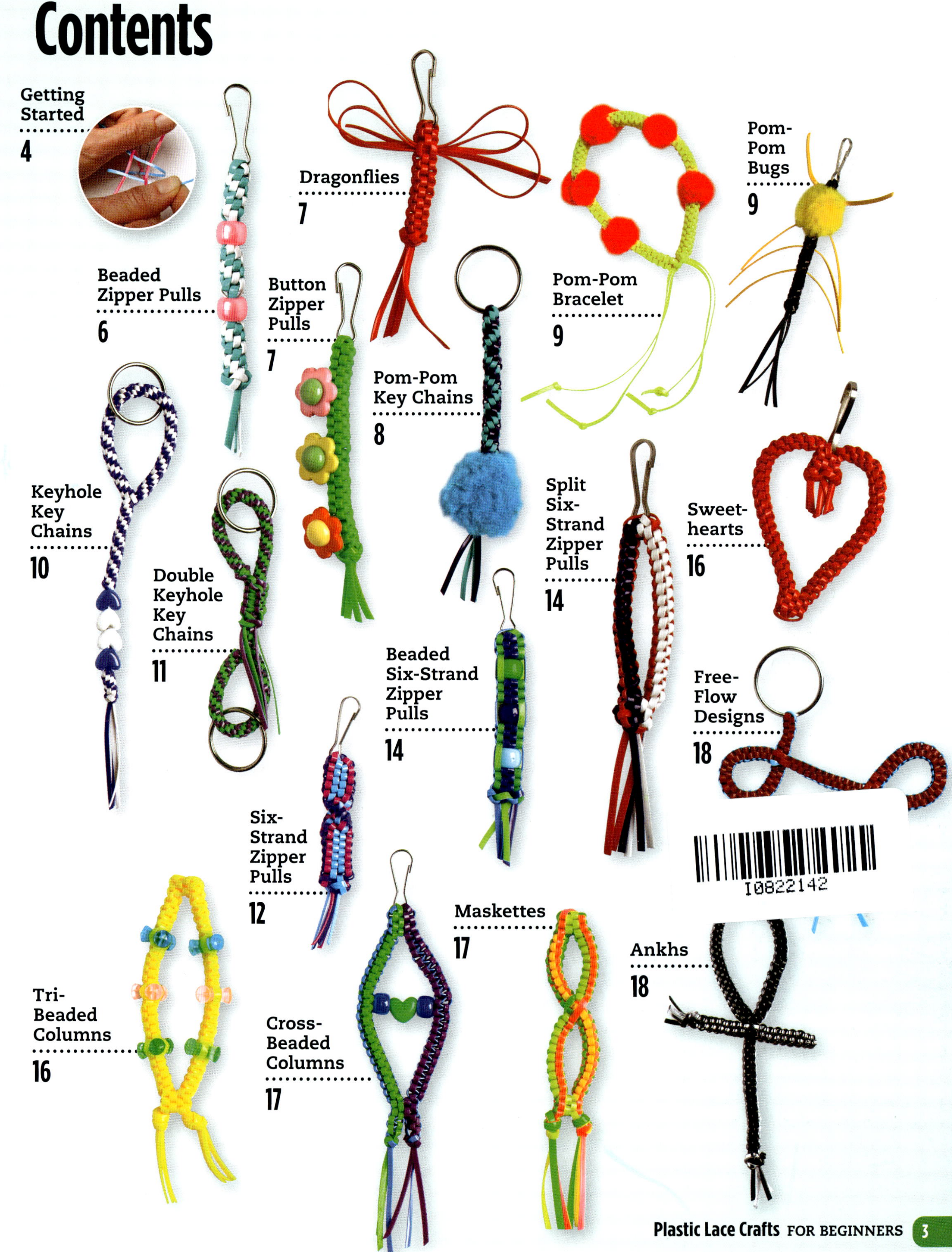

Getting Started

Beginning a Four-Strand Project

1 Thread two strands of plastic lace through a lanyard hook until the hook is at the middle of the laces. To practice, start with 24-inch pieces. Fasten down with a piece of tape for the first stitch; remove tape after step **5**.

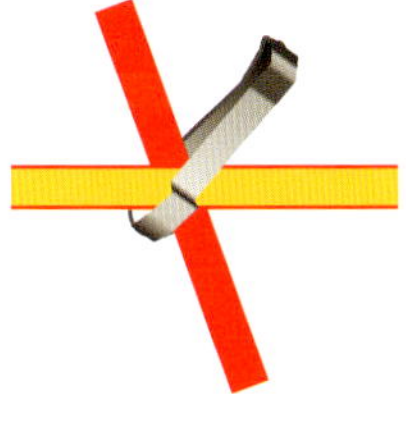

2 Fold one end back.

3 Fold the next end over it.

4 Fold the third end over the second.

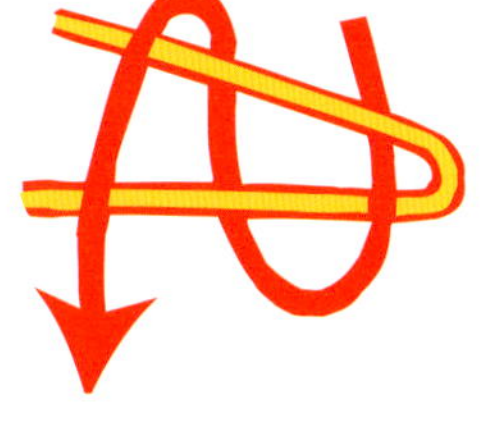

5 Fold the fourth end over the third and under the loop formed by the first fold.

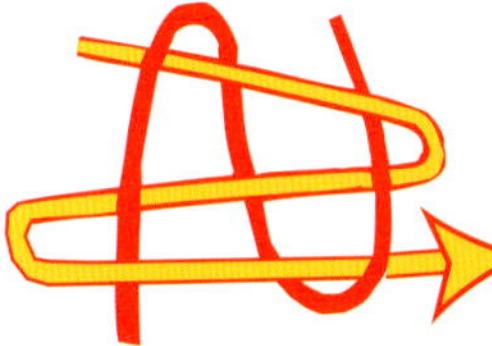

6 Remove the tape, and pull the stitch tight.

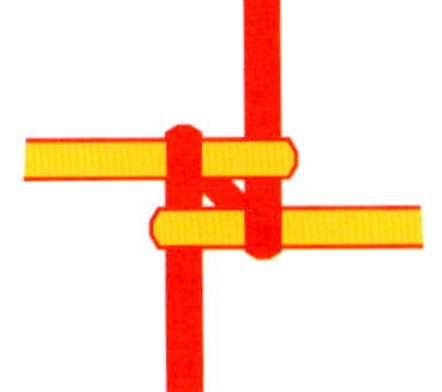

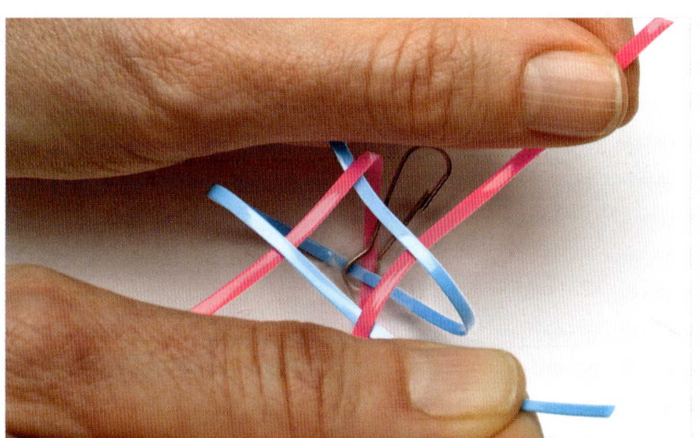

Here you can see the first stitch with the lace still taped down (step **5**).

A regular stitch will look like this before you tighten it (step **10a**).

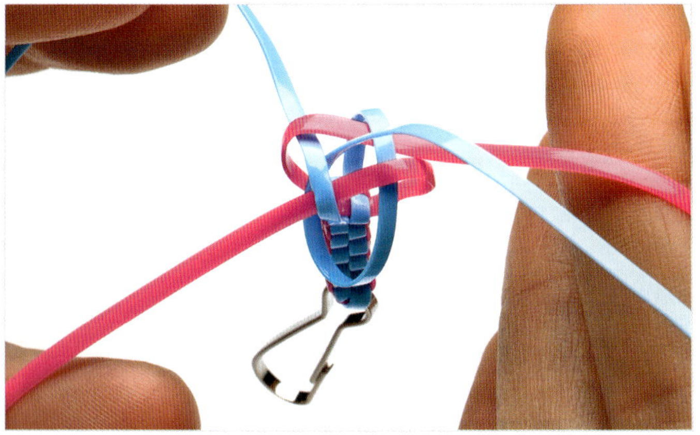

When finishing a project, you will thread each strand up through the square formed by the loose final stitch (step **12**).

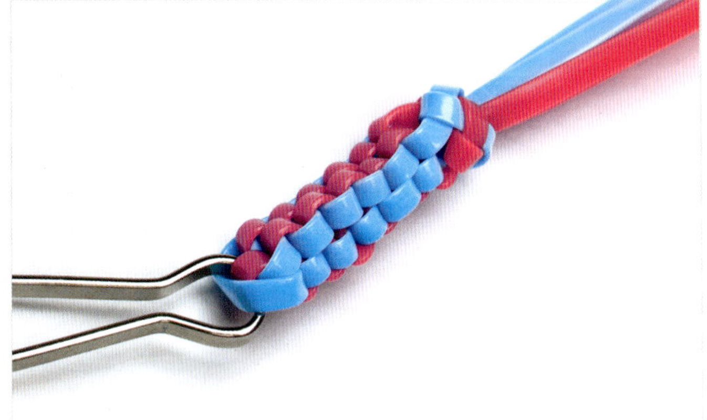

Your finished four-strand project will look something like this.

The Square Stitch

7a To make a square stitch, fold the first strand over itself.

8a Fold the other laces one at a time, starting here with the second lace.

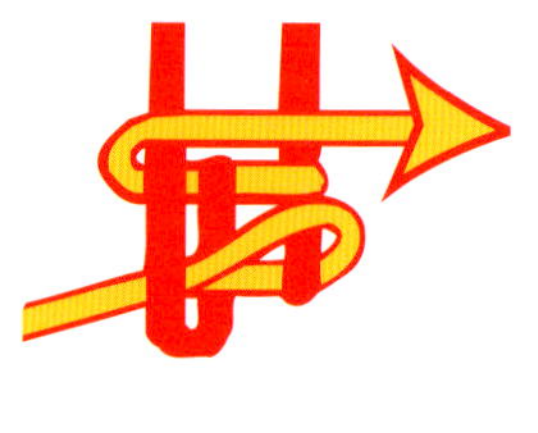

9a Fold the third lace.

10a Fold the fourth lace, making sure to thread it under the loop formed by the first lace.

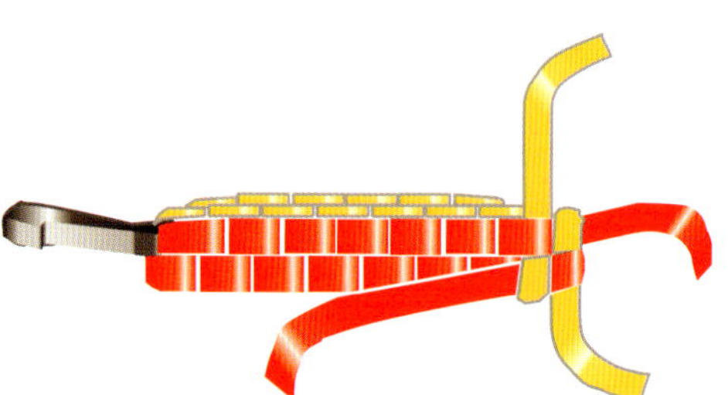

11a Tighten. As you continue making square stitches, the box pattern will appear.

The Round Stitch

7b To make a round stitch, fold the first strand over the opposite one, at an angle.

8b Fold the adjacent strand over it, again at an angle.

9b Fold the third strand.

10b Fold the fourth strand, making sure to thread it through the loop of the first strand.

11b Tighten; the stitch is rotated from the first. Make the second and succeeding stitches the same as the first—if it went clockwise, continue clockwise; if it went counterclockwise, continue counterclockwise. As you continue making round stitches, the spiral pattern will appear.

Finishing

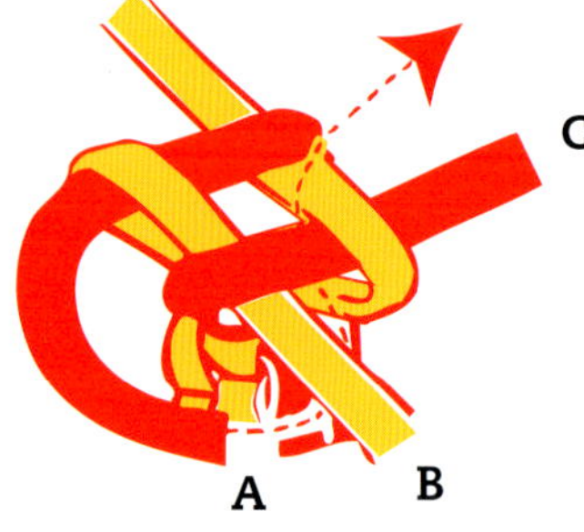

12 To finish your project, make a final square stitch, and leave it loose. Run strand A under strand B and up through the center. Run strand B under C and up the center. Continue with C and D, so all ends are together in the center. Now pull tight, and trim off the ends at the desired length.

Beaded Zipper Pulls

Materials

- 2 pieces 24-inch plastic lace
- Pony beads or heart beads
- 1 lanyard hook

It's quite simple to add a variety of beads to a stitched zipper pull. You can create a variety of designs, too.

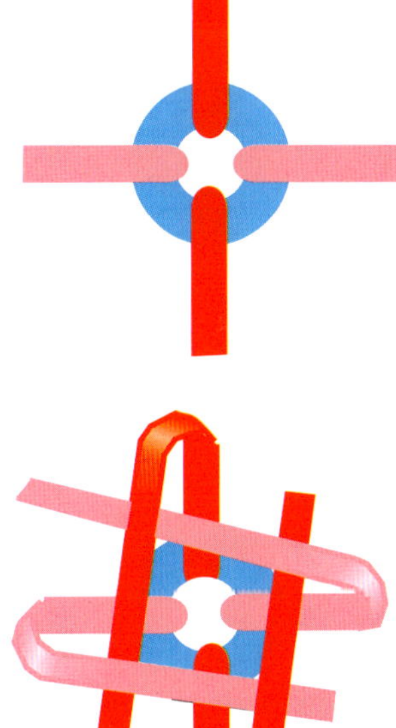

1 For a simple **Pony Bead Zipper Pull**, start off with nine square stitches, and then thread all four ends through a pony bead. When they emerge from the pony bead, spread the ends out so that two of the same color are opposite each other.

2 Proceed to make a new square stitch. After five square stitches, thread the four ends through a second pony bead. Make five or six more square stitches. You may finish in the usual way, or run the four strands through a third pony bead, then run two strands through a second time.

Pony Bead

Kissing Heart

Caged Bead

For the **Kissing Heart Bead Zipper Pull**, start with nine round stitches. Thread all four ends through one heart bead, base first, then through a second heart bead, tip first. After they emerge from the second bead, make nine more stitches and finish.

For the **Caged Bead Zipper Pull**, start with four round or square stitches. Pull them very tight. Make two more stitches, and leave them loose. Take a pony bead, insert it into the cage of the first stitch, and tighten the cage around it by pulling tight the second stitch. Make four more very tight stitches. Again make two loose stitches, insert a pony bead inside the first one, and tighten the second one around it. Repeat the process once or twice, so that you have three or four caged pony beads. After four additional stitches, finish and trim.

Button Zipper Pulls

Materials

- 2 pieces 24-inch plastic lace
- 1–3 buttons
- 1 lanyard hook

Buttons come with small loops, large loops, or holes in them. If they come with small loops, like the **dinosaur** and **flowers**, just run a strand through the loop wherever you want the button placed, and continue stitching. If there is a large loop, run all four strands through it, and pick up the stitch on the far side as with the pony bead on page 6. If there are holes in the bead, run one or two strands through, and continue stitching.

Dragonflies

Materials

- 2 pieces 24- (red) or 36- (yellow) inch plastic lace
- 1 piece 18- (red) or 24- (yellow) inch plastic lace for wings
- 1 lanyard hook

Start the basic zipper pull, and make three tight round or square stitches. Make two loose stitches. Take the short piece of plastic lace and bend it back and forth in 2½-inch (red) to 3-inch (yellow) loops, so that you have two loops on each side. Pinch one side to narrow it, insert it into the first loose stitch until it is halfway through, and quickly tighten the two stitches. Continue stitching for another inch (red) to 1½ inches (yellow), and finish.

Pom-Pom Key Chains

Materials

- 2 pieces 36-inch plastic lace
- 1 pom-pom (1–1½ inch)
- 1 lanyard hook or mini-ring
- 1 pony or heart bead

Start a four-strand project with a square or round stitch, and continue until you have laced 2 inches. If you have pom-pom beads, just thread the lace through the center of the bead. If you have regular pom-poms, follow the step-by-step directions.

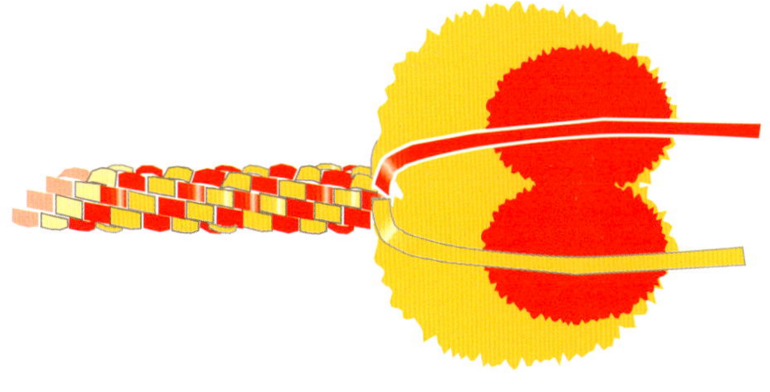

1 Find the string in the center of the pom-pom, and with the end of a paper clip work the pom-pom into two halves by following the string around the pom-pom center. Run two strands of different colors in the groove on opposite sides of the pom-pom.

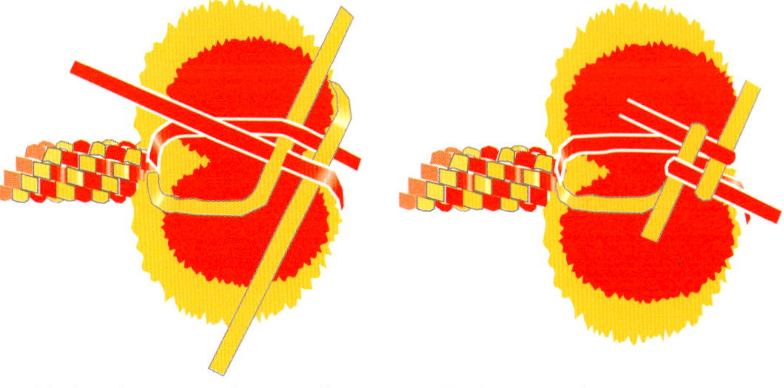

2 Unite the strands together in a stitch.

3 Tighten with one more square or round stitch, and finish the project.

For the **zig-zag pattern** with the turquoise pom-pom, after eight round stitches, make one square stitch to reverse the direction of the spiral. Continue with the 8:1 pattern all the way.

Instructions for inserting a bead are on page 6. To enliven your pom-pom, glue on wiggle eyes and a bead for its mouth.

Pom-Pom Bracelet

Materials

- 2 pieces 7-foot plastic lace
- 5 small pom-poms (½–¾ inch)
- 1 large paper clip

Anchor the two strands on a paper clip, and do square stitches for 1 inch. Do not remove the paper clip. Attach a pom-pom as on page 8. Continue attaching pom-poms at 1-inch intervals until five are in place. Make a final inch of square stitches. The finishing design will allow you to slip the bracelet on and then tighten it; follow the step-by-step illustrations.

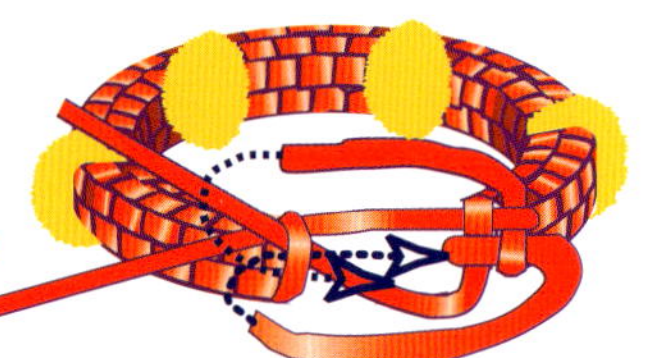

1 Remove the paper clip, which leaves an X from the initial crossover. Take two adjacent strands and pass them through the X from one side.

2 Take the other two strands, and pass them under the X from the other side. Tie an overhand knot in each strand 2 ½ inches out, and trim. For a nice variation, pass the four ends through a pony bead before knotting; this will hold them more snugly.

Pom-Pom Bugs

Materials

- 2 pieces 36-inch plastic lace
- 1 pom-pom
- 1 lanyard hook
- 4 pieces 3- to 4-inch plastic lace or chenille stems

For this project, you will start as with a regular four-strand project and add bug body parts as you go along. For the antennae, after three stitches lay a short piece of lace or chenille stem across the center of the square, and stitch over it (**A**). After two further stitches, enclose the pom-pom as before (Pom-Pom Key Chains steps **1–3**). After four more stitches, it's time for the legs! Lay the second short piece across the center, parallel to the first. Insects must have six legs! After eight more stitches, in goes the second set, and after a further eight stitches, attach the third set. Make seven more stitches and finish off. With the chenille stems, add the realistic touches: bend the antennae up and then forward; bend the legs down and their tips forward.

To add the antennae, lay a short piece of lace or chenille stem across the center of the last stitch, and stitch over it.

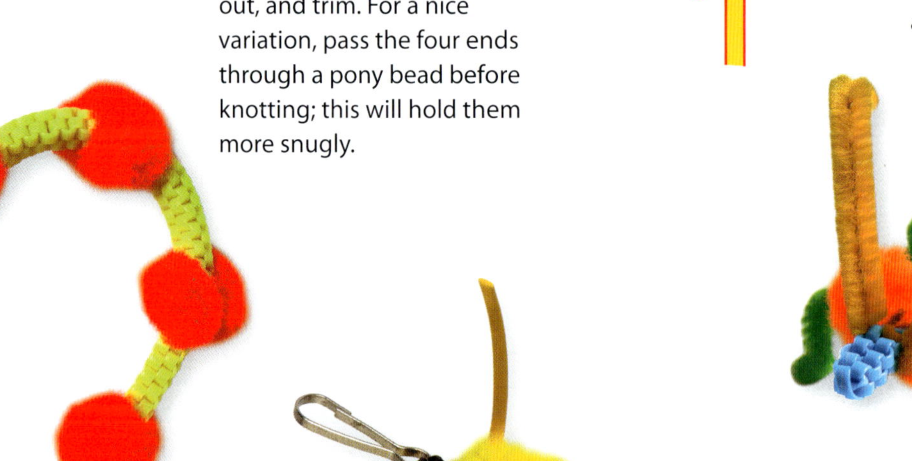

Keyhole Key Chains

Materials

- 2 pieces 6-foot plastic lace
- 1 key ring

Start this project like any normal four-strand project with round or square stitches. Continue making stitches until you have made about 5 inches. You have a simple, straight project. Now dive into the step-by-step instructions to make the keyhole.

1 Remove the ring from the end and slip it over the woven part. If you look at the end, you will see two laces crossed in an X.

2 Loop the woven part back on itself so the working end touches the finished end. Slip the two closest strands through the X so that each goes under its own color strand.

3 Make another stitch, pulling it tight to join the two ends. As you continue making stitches, you will see that they have made a slight angle with the loop. Continue for another two inches or so and finish off. For variety, add some pony or heart beads or a pom-pom.

Double Keyhole Key Chains

Materials

- 2 pieces 9-foot plastic lace
- 2 key rings

1 After following the steps to create a Keyhole Key Chain and bringing the two ends together (Keyhole Key Chains step **3**), proceed making stitches for about 7 inches. Slip a second ring over the end, and bring it around to form a loop with itself about 1 ½ inches from the joining of the first loop.

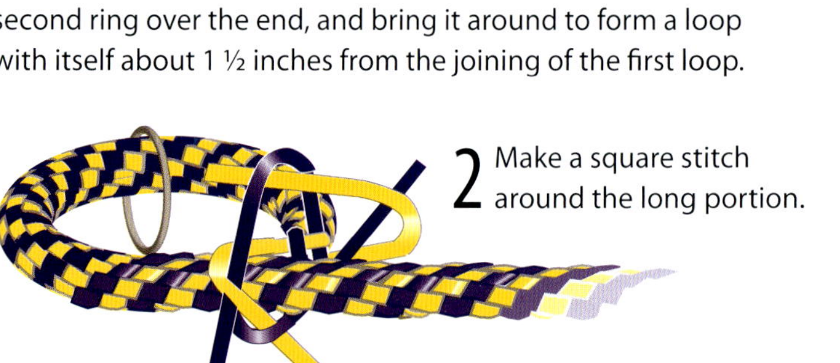

2 Make a square stitch around the long portion.

3 Pull the stitch tight.

4 Continue with square stitches until you have made about eight, and the new loop is securely in place.

5 Finish off in the usual manner; now when each strand comes up the center, it will be alongside the central column.

Six-Strand Zipper Pulls

Materials

- 1 piece 38-inch plastic lace
- 2 pieces 32-inch plastic lace
- 1 lanyard hook

You can achieve many more cool shapes and effects by using six strands instead of four. Here are the basics of six-strand projects. They are more complicated than four-strand projects, but follow the same general techniques.

Beginning a Six-Strand Project

1 Thread the three pieces of plastic lace through the lanyard hook until it is at the center of each of them; cross the two shorter pieces. It doesn't matter which is in front. Fasten in place with pieces of tape for the first stitch; remove tape before step **7**.

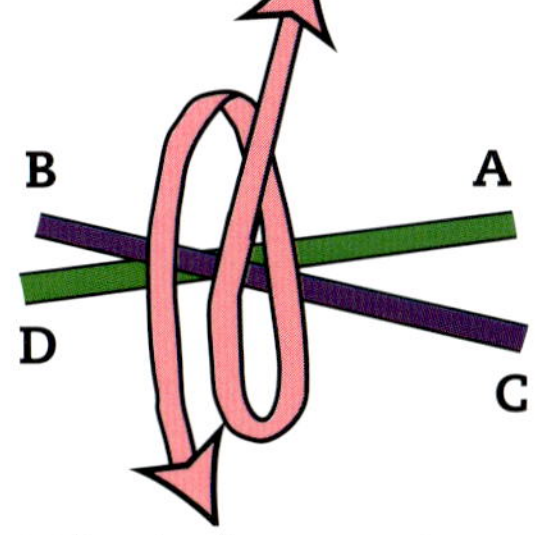

2 Take the longest piece and fold over to form the guidelines. Keep them parallel; do not allow them to cross.

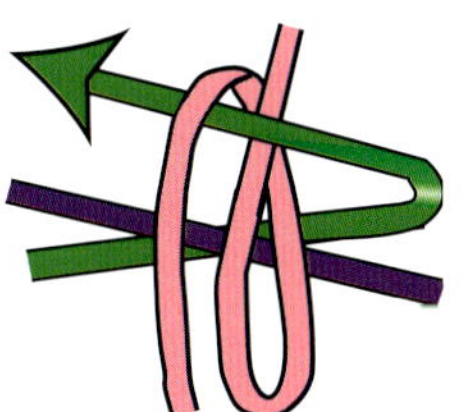

3 Following the arrows, place A (green) over the first guideline and under the loop of the second guideline.

4 Similarly, place B (violet) over the near guideline and under the far guideline.

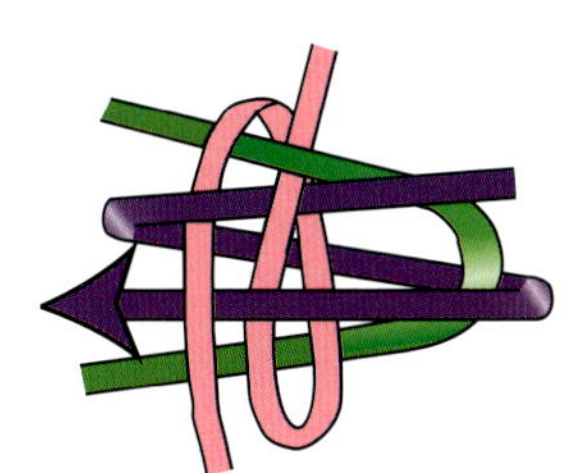

5 Next, place C (violet) over the near and under the far guideline.

6 Finally, place D (green) over the near guideline and under the loop of the far guideline.

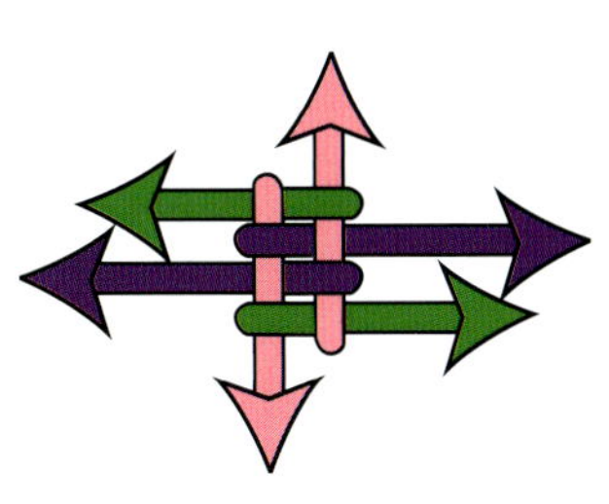

7 The stitch is complete; remove the tape fasteners, pull tight in the direction of the arrows, and see the symmetrical pattern.

The Straight Stitch (8a–12a)

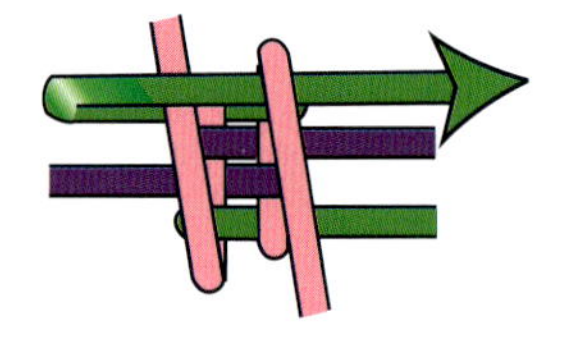

8a A straight stitch is made similar to this by folding the two guideline laces straight back over themselves, and placing each lace in succession over the near guideline and under the far one (**9a–11a**).

9a Following the arrows, place the top green strand over the first guideline and under the loop of the second guideline.

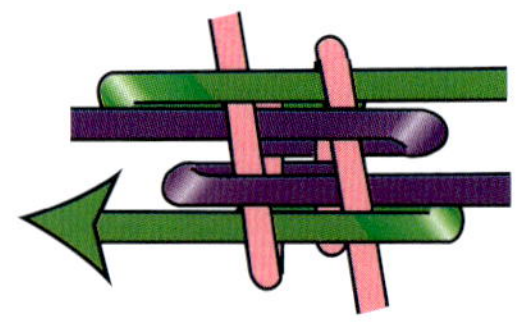

10a Similarly, place the middle violet strands over the near guidelines and under the far guidelines.

11a Finally, place the bottom green strand over the near guideline and under the loop of the far guideline.

12a When you pull tight, you will see that the outside color remains outside, and the inside color stays inside. Continue straight stitches for 2 inches to make colorful **Straight** zipper pulls; finish as shown below in step **13**.

The Spiral Stitch (8b–12b)

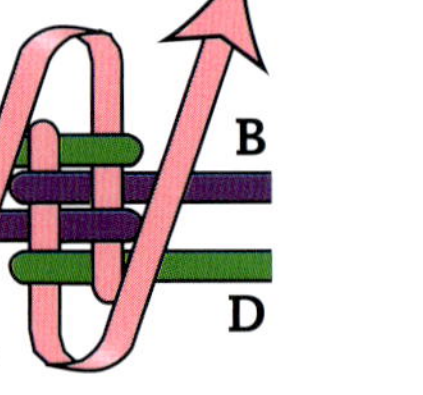

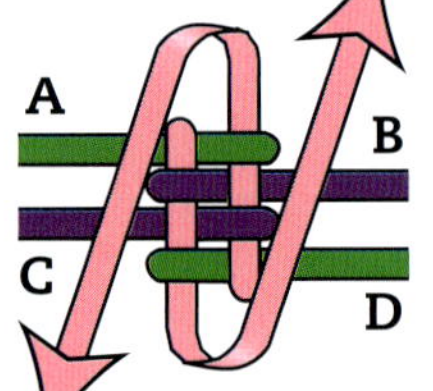

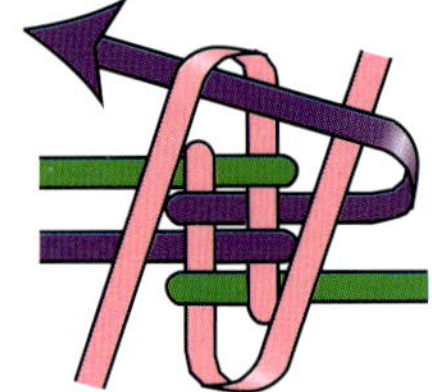

8b To start the spiral stitch, fold the guideline laces on an angle.

9b Place the second lace B over the near guideline and under the loop of the far guideline.

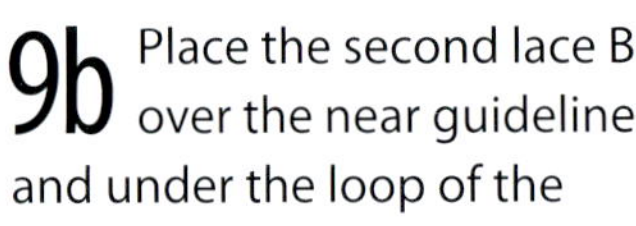

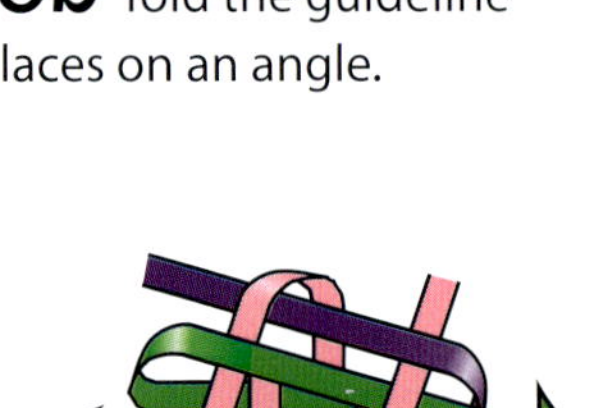

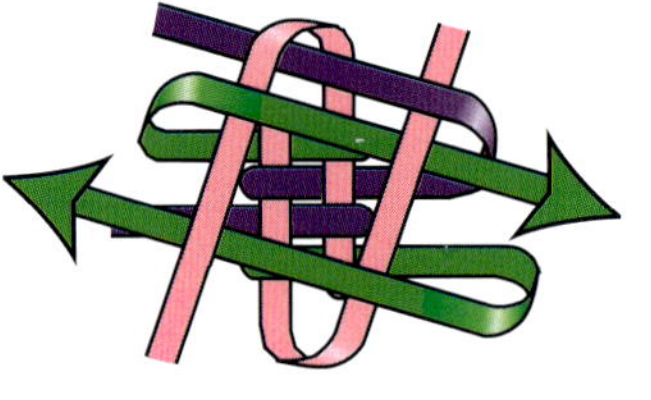

10b Place the first lace A and the last lace D over the near and under the far guideline.

11b Finally, place the third lace C over the near guideline and under the loop of the far guideline.

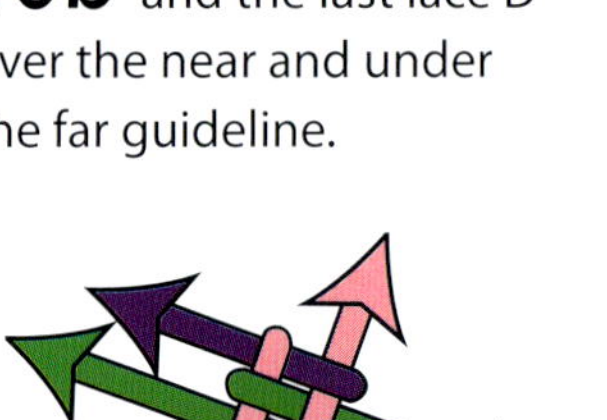

12b When you pull the spiral stitch tight, you will see that the outside and inside colors have reversed places! They will continue to do so with each spiral stitch.

After 2 inches, a spiral stitch project will look like the small **Spiral** key chain. An odd number of straight stitches will reverse the direction of a spiral; an even number of straight stitches continues the spiral in the same sense as before. For the **Flare**, stitch 10 straight, 6 spiral, and 10 straight, or make 12 spiral stitches for a double flare.

Finishing

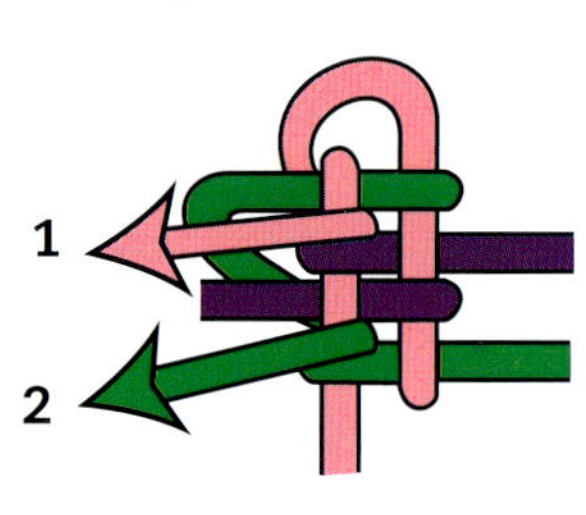

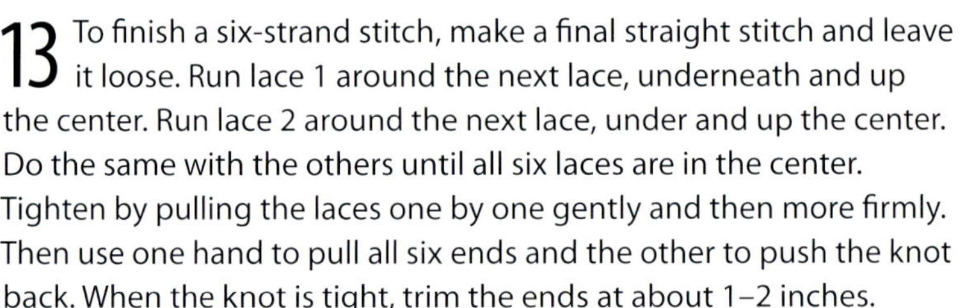

13 To finish a six-strand stitch, make a final straight stitch and leave it loose. Run lace 1 around the next lace, underneath and up the center. Run lace 2 around the next lace, under and up the center. Do the same with the others until all six laces are in the center. Tighten by pulling the laces one by one gently and then more firmly. Then use one hand to pull all six ends and the other to push the knot back. When the knot is tight, trim the ends at about 1–2 inches.

Beaded Six-Strand Zipper Pulls

Materials

- 1 piece 38-inch plastic lace
- 2 pieces 32-inch plastic lace
- 3 pony beads
- 1 lanyard hook

1 Start a basic Six-Strand Zipper Pull, and make four square stitches. Thread the two central strands through a pony bead, and spread them apart.

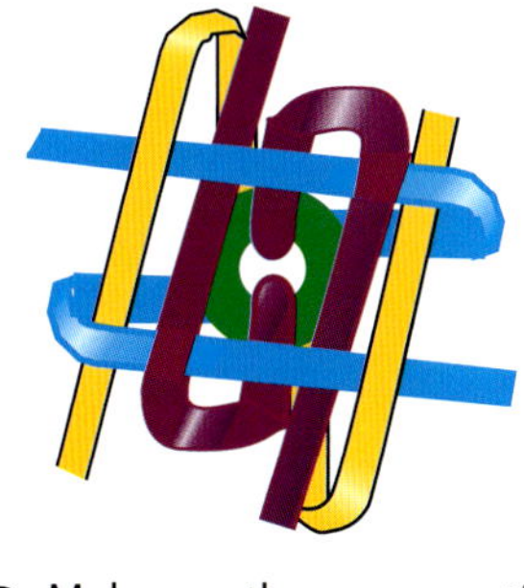

2 Make another square stitch, continue with a second one, and pull tight. Note that 4 strands are outside the pony bead, lightly touching it. After four stitches, run the two central strands through a second pony bead; after four more stitches, run them through a third bead. Complete with four final stiches, and finish off.

Split Six-Strand Zipper Pulls

Materials

- 3 pieces 30- to 36-inch plastic lace
- 1 lanyard hook

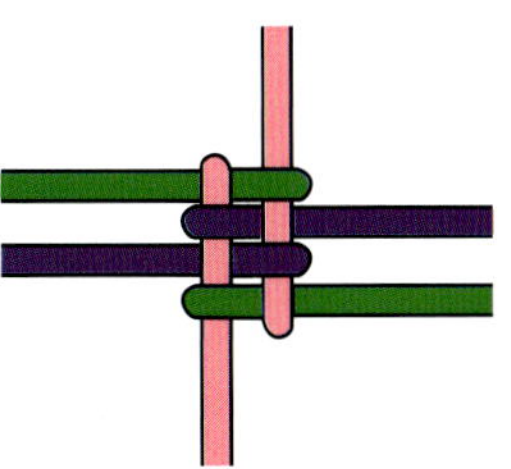

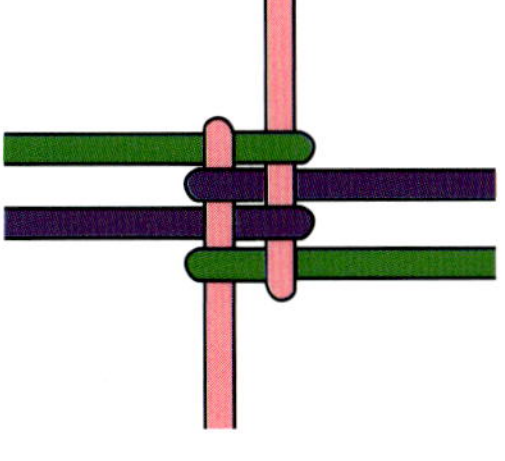

1 Start a Six-Strand Zipper Pull using the square stitch. After you have completed four stitches, separate the three strands on one end from the three on the other.

2 Stitch each group of three in either a **straight** or **angled** stitch. For the **straight** stitch, run one strand back over itself.

3 Run the next strand over it.

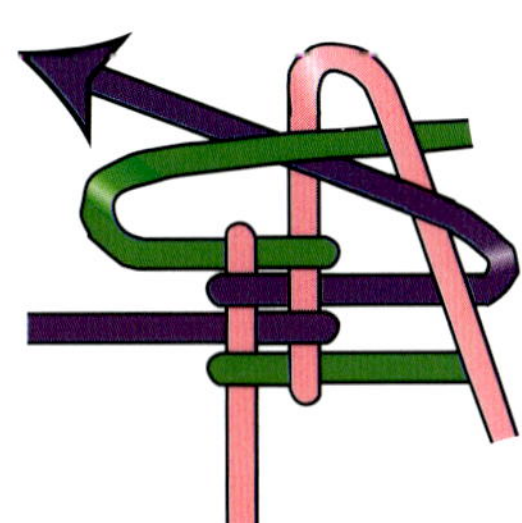

4 Complete the stitch by running the third strand over the second and under the loop of the first strand.

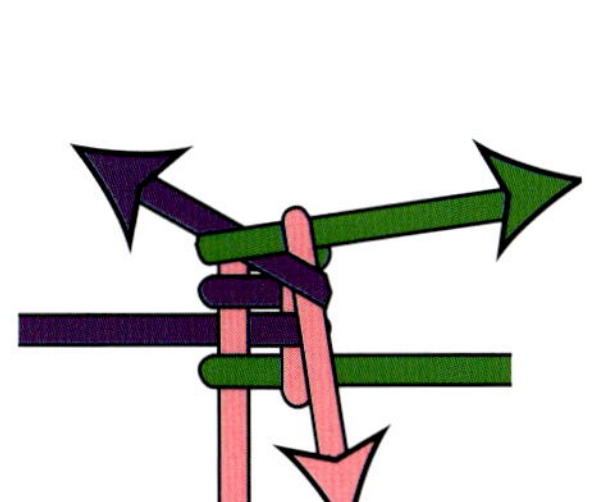

5 Pull tight, and see the triangular form take shape.

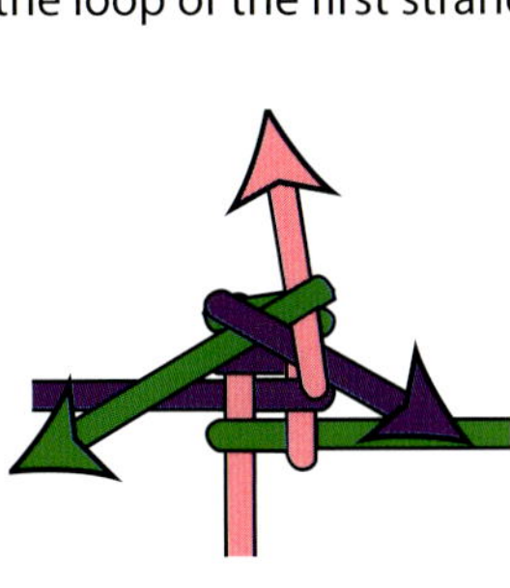

6 To continue, keep folding each strand over itself. Use the same stitch on the other group of three, the same number of times.

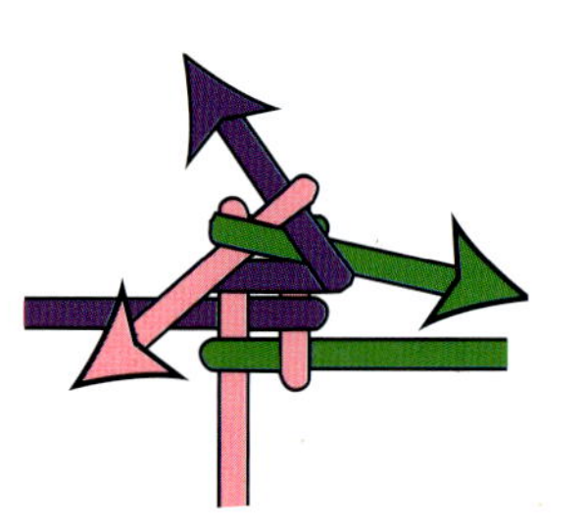

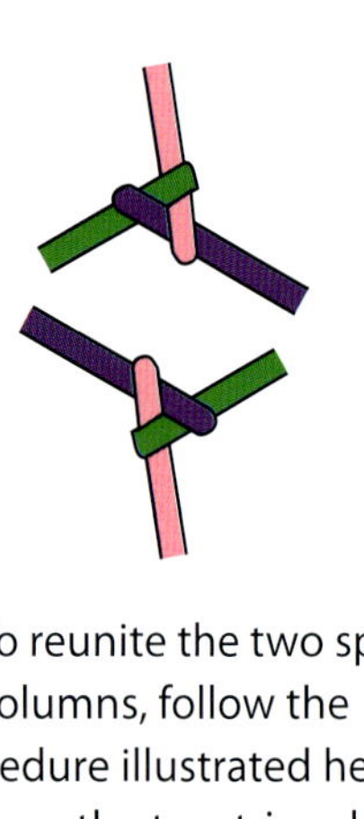

7 For the **angled** stitch, each strand is run over the neighboring strand instead of over itself. The resulting spiral is very gentle (about one rotation in 2 inches), and with a slight twist it can be made straight! For all of these zipper pulls, you can use either stitch.

8 To reunite the two split columns, follow the procedure illustrated here. Arrange the two triangles so the long end strands are pointing away from each other.

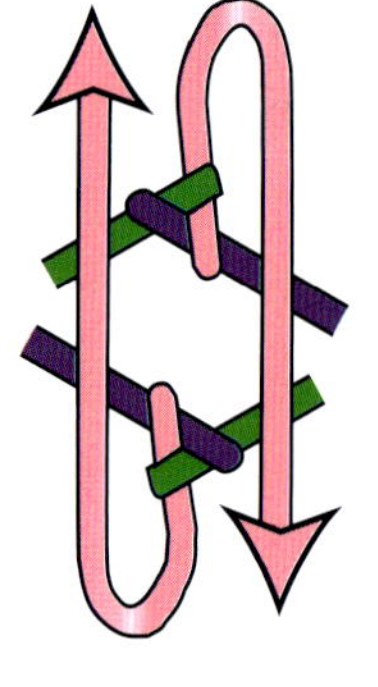

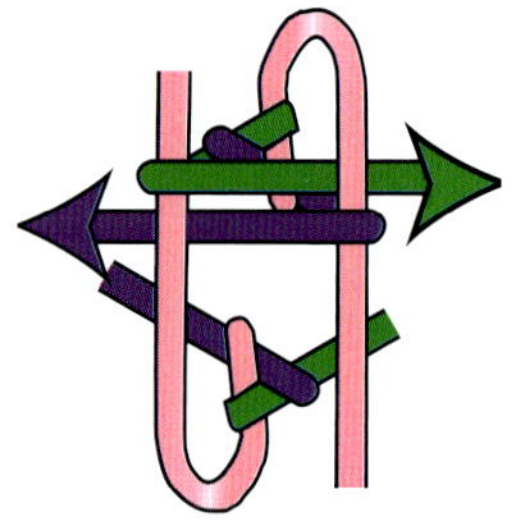

9 Fold them back to form the guidelines.

10 Fold the outside and then the inside strands of one triangle over and under their respective guidelines.

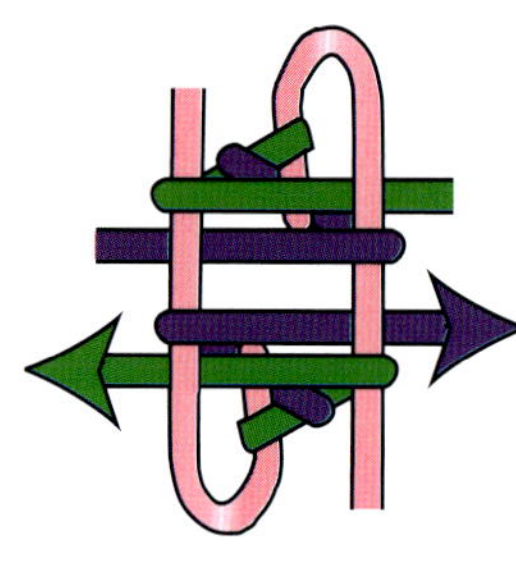

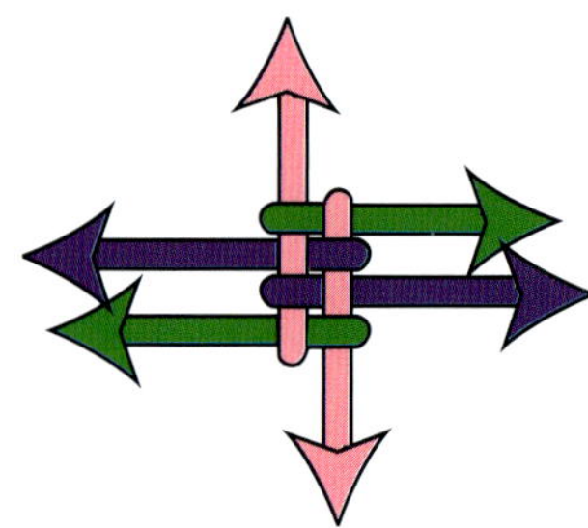

11 Do the same with two strands of the second triangle.

12 Pull all ends tight, as they were in the original Six-Strand Zipper Pull. Continue for two stitches. You can finish directly (**Basic Split**), or split again to form a fishtail, and finish the three-ends just as you do four or six ends (**Split and Fishtail**).

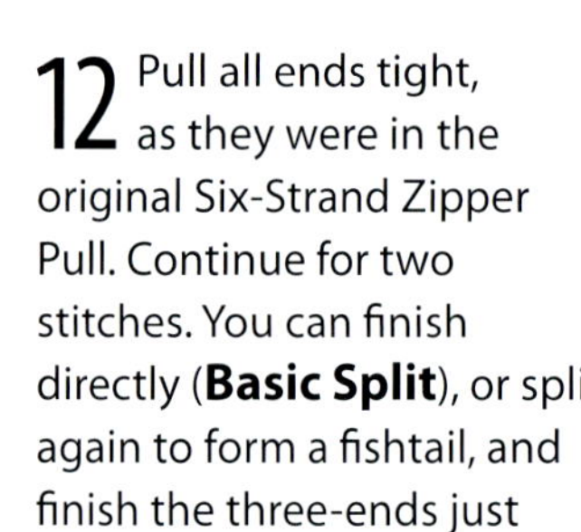

Split and Fishtail

Basic Split

Sweethearts

Materials

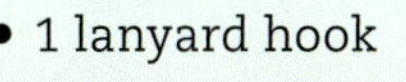

- 3 pieces 36- to 60-inch plastic lace
- 1 lanyard hook

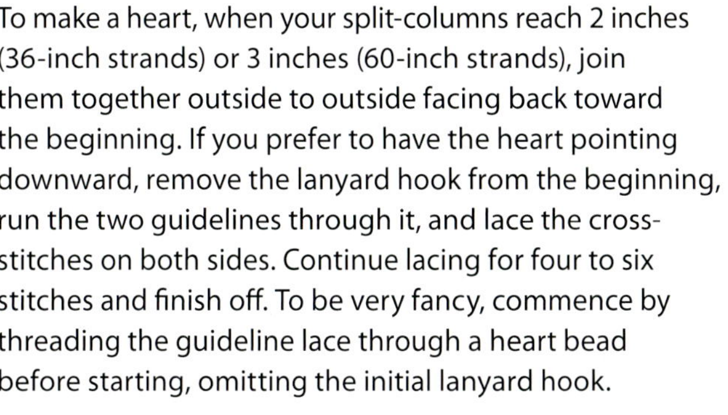

To make a heart, when your split-columns reach 2 inches (36-inch strands) or 3 inches (60-inch strands), join them together outside to outside facing back toward the beginning. If you prefer to have the heart pointing downward, remove the lanyard hook from the beginning, run the two guidelines through it, and lace the cross-stitches on both sides. Continue lacing for four to six stitches and finish off. To be very fancy, commence by threading the guideline lace through a heart bead before starting, omitting the initial lanyard hook.

Tri-Beaded Columns

Materials

- 3 pieces 36-inch plastic lace
- 6 tri-beads
- 1 lanyard hook

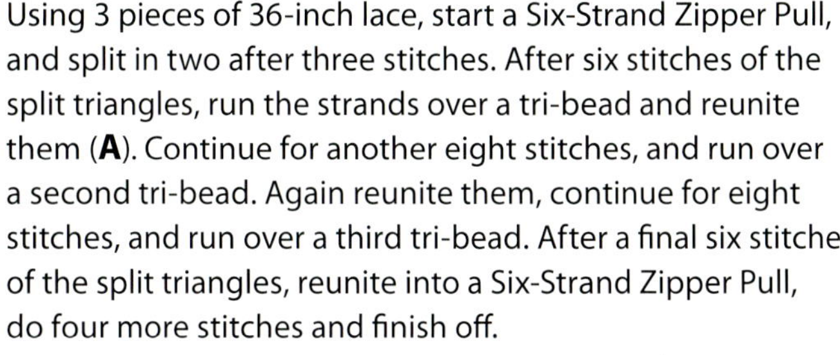

Using 3 pieces of 36-inch lace, start a Six-Strand Zipper Pull, and split in two after three stitches. After six stitches of the split triangles, run the strands over a tri-bead and reunite them (**A**). Continue for another eight stitches, and run over a second tri-bead. Again reunite them, continue for eight stitches, and run over a third tri-bead. After a final six stitches of the split triangles, reunite into a Six-Strand Zipper Pull, do four more stitches and finish off.

Cross-Beaded Columns

Materials
- 3 pieces 36- to 60-inch plastic lace
- 1–3 beads
- 1 lanyard hook

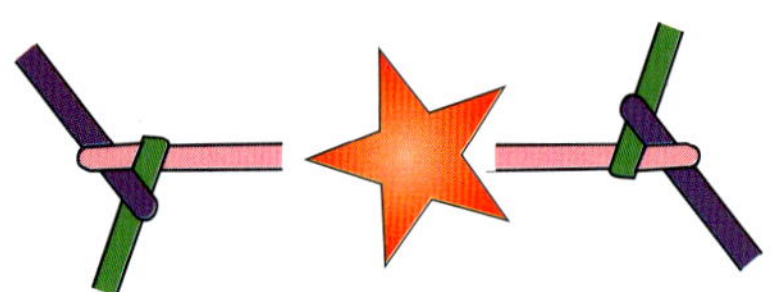

1 Start a Six-Strand Zipper Pull, and split in two after three stitches. After eight stitches of the split triangles, arrange the triangles so the long end strands are pointing toward each other.

2 Run them through the bead or beads in opposite directions.

3 Continue with the triangular stitch. You can repeat this once more if you want two cross-beads. After a final eight stitches, reunite the two triangles into a Six-Strand Zipper Pull.

If you wish to add the teddy bear or a single set of beads, make 16 stitches of the split triangle first, then add the beads, then make a final 16 triangle stitches. After reuniting into a Six-Strand Zipper Pull, make four to six stitches and finish off.

Maskettes

Materials
- 3 pieces 30- to 36-inch plastic lace
- 1 lanyard hook

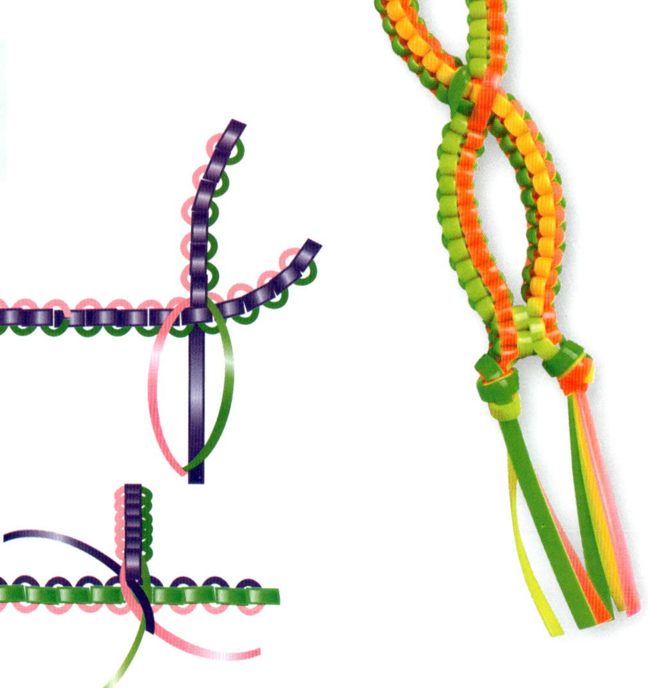

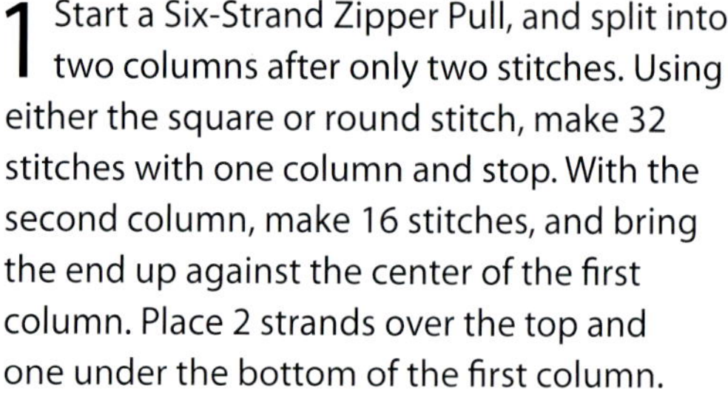

1 Start a Six-Strand Zipper Pull, and split into two columns after only two stitches. Using either the square or round stitch, make 32 stitches with one column and stop. With the second column, make 16 stitches, and bring the end up against the center of the first column. Place 2 strands over the top and one under the bottom of the first column.

2 Make a stitch on the other side, pull it tight, and proceed to make another 16 stitches. Reunite into a single Six-Strand Zipper Pull, make two further stitches, and finish off.

Ankhs

Materials

- 2 pieces 6-foot plastic lace
- 2 pieces 20-inch plastic lace
- 1 key ring

The Ankh was the ancient Egyptian symbol for life and vitality. It is found in the name of the famous boy-king, Tut-ankh-amen (**above**). Make one, and use it as a lively pin or pull or chain.

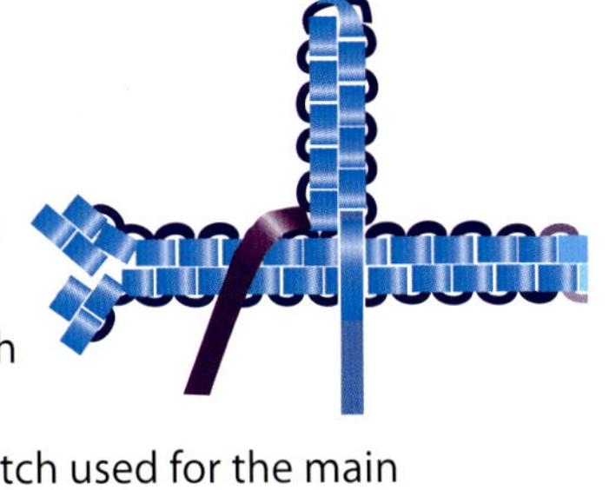

1 Start a Keyhole Key Chain as on page 10. (If you wish to make a pin or pull, leave out the ring.) Finish the straight section after 2 inches. For the cross-arm, take 20 inches of each of the two colors already used, and start stitching the same stitch used for the main body of the Ankh. After nine stitches, run two strands over and two under the straight section.

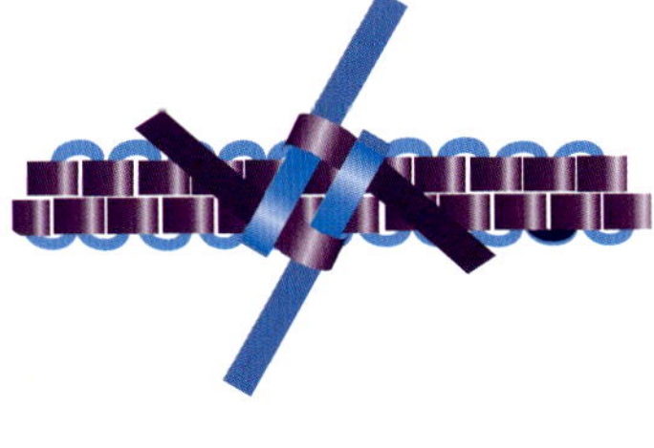

2 Close with a stitch on the other side. Slide the cross-arm near to the loop and tighten. Continue with eight more stitches, finish, and cut the ends close.

Free-Flow Designs

Materials

- 1–2 pieces 7-foot or longer plastic lace
- 1 lanyard hook

Use the crossover technique of the Ankh to generate a free-flow design. Shown is an idea with just one long stitch turning and crossing itself in different directions. Another option is to start a whole new length of stitches with new lace, crossing the lengths as many times as you want, and combining the lengths at the end. You can end with pony beads. Get imaginative and try your own designs.